Table of Contents

INTRODUCTION

I welcome you all to the world of "Protein-Packed Palate: A Cookbook for a Protein-Rich Lifestyle"! In a world where health-conscious eating has become more than just a trend, this cookbook is your ultimate guide to nourishing your body with the power of protein. Whether you're an athlete looking to optimize performance, a fitness enthusiast aiming to build muscle, or simply someone who values a balanced and wholesome diet, this cookbook is here to transform your culinary journey.

The Importance of Protein:

Protein is often referred to as the building block of life, and for good reason. It plays a crucial role in various bodily functions, from repairing tissues and supporting immune function to producing enzymes and hormones. Including an adequate amount of protein in your diet can help you feel fuller for longer, promote muscle growth and repair, boost metabolism, and stabilize blood sugar levels.

Embracing a Protein-Rich Lifestyle:

In "Protein-Packed Palate," I've meticulously curated a collection of recipes that celebrate the diverse and delicious ways you can incorporate protein-rich ingredients into your meals. From breakfast to dinner, and even snacks, I've got you covered. My recipes encompass a variety of protein sources, including lean meats, poultry, fish, dairy products, legumes, nuts, seeds, and plant-based alternatives.

Cookbook Highlights:

Breakfast Boosters: Kickstart your day with protein-packed breakfast options that go beyond the traditional eggs and bacon. Discover delightful quinoa breakfast bowls, Greek yogurt parfaits, and protein smoothies that will keep you energized all morning long.

Wholesome Lunches: Transform your midday meal with creative salads, wraps, and bowls featuring grilled chicken, chickpeas, tofu, and more. These recipes are designed to keep you satisfied and focused throughout the day.

Hearty Dinners: Elevate your evening dining experience with an array of protein-rich dishes. Indulge in savory lentil stews, succulent fish fillets, and lean beef stir-fries that make dinnertime both nutritious and flavorful.

Snack Smart: Bid farewell to empty-calorie snacks and explore our protein-rich snack ideas. From roasted chickpeas to homemade protein bars, these snacks will curb cravings and provide a lasting energy boost.

Sweet Sensations: Yes, even desserts can be protein-rich! Indulge guilt-free in treats like chocolate protein pancakes, chia seed puddings, and nut butter-infused cookies that satisfy your sweet tooth without sacrificing nutrition.

Cooking Tips and Techniques:

"Protein-Packed Palate" isn't just a collection of recipes — it's a comprehensive guide to mastering protein-rich cooking. Throughout the book, you'll find cooking tips, substitution suggestions, and insights into optimizing the nutritional value of your meals. Learn how to marinate proteins effectively, cook grains for maximum protein absorption, and balance flavors for a truly exceptional dining experience.

Get ready to embark on a culinary adventure that combines the joy of cooking with the science of nutrition. "Protein-Packed Palate" is your passport to a healthier, more vibrant you. So, grab your apron, sharpen those knives, and let's dive into a world of protein-rich deliciousness that will leave you satisfied, energized, and excited about the possibilities of your kitchen.

PROTEIN RICH DIET COOKBOOK

BREAKFAST

1. Greek Yogurt Parfait:

Ingredients:

- Greek yogurt

- Mixed berries (blueberries, strawberries, raspberries)

- Granola

- Honey

Instructions:

- In a glass or bowl, layer Greek yogurt.

- Add a layer of mixed berries.

- Sprinkle granola over the berries.

- Drizzle honey on top.

- Repeat the layers if desired.

2. Spinach and Feta Scramble:

Ingredients:

- Eggs

- Spinach

- Feta cheese

- Salt and pepper

- Olive oil

Instructions:

- Heat olive oil in a pan over medium heat.

- Add spinach and sauté until wilted.

- In a bowl, whisk eggs and season with salt and pepper.

- Pour the eggs into the pan with spinach.

- Cook and scramble until eggs are set.

- Sprinkle feta cheese over the top before serving.

3. Oatmeal with Almond Butter and Banana:

Ingredients:

• Rolled oats

• Almond butter

• Banana

• Almonds (optional)

• Cinnamon

Instructions:

• Cook oats according to package instructions.

• Top with a spoonful of almond butter.

• Slice a banana and place on top.

• Sprinkle with almonds and a dash of cinnamon.

4. Quinoa Breakfast Bowl:

Ingredients:

• Cooked quinoa

- Mixed nuts (walnuts, almonds, etc.)

- Dried fruits (raisins, apricots, etc.)

- Milk (dairy or plant-based)

Instructions:

- Mix cooked quinoa with mixed nuts and dried fruits.

- Pour milk over the mixture.

- Warm in the microwave if desired.

5. Cottage Cheese Pancakes:

Ingredients:

- Cottage cheese

- Eggs

- Whole wheat flour

- Baking powder

- Vanilla extract

Instructions:

• Blend cottage cheese, eggs, flour, baking powder, and vanilla extract in a blender.

• Pour batter onto a heated non-stick pan to make pancakes.

• Cook until bubbles form, then flip and cook the other side.

6. Breakfast Burrito:

Ingredients:

• Whole wheat tortilla

• Scrambled eggs

• Black beans

• Salsa

• Avocado

Instructions:

- Warm the tortilla.

- Fill with scrambled eggs, black beans, salsa, and avocado.

- Roll into a burrito and enjoy.

7. Chia Seed Pudding:

Ingredients:

- Chia seeds

- Milk (dairy or plant-based)

- Vanilla extract

- Honey

- Fresh fruits

Instructions:

- Mix chia seeds, milk, vanilla extract, and honey in a bowl.

- Let it sit in the refrigerator overnight to thicken.

- Top with fresh fruits before serving.

8. Protein Smoothie:

Ingredients:

- Protein powder (whey or plant-based)

- Frozen berries

- Banana

- Spinach

- Milk or water

Instructions:

- Blend protein powder, frozen berries, banana, spinach, and liquid until smooth.

9. Egg and Veggie Muffins:

Ingredients:

- Eggs

- Chopped vegetables (bell peppers, spinach, tomatoes, etc.)

- Cheese (optional)

- Salt and pepper

Instructions:

- Preheat oven and grease muffin tin.

- Beat eggs, add chopped vegetables, cheese, salt, and pepper.

- Pour mixture into muffin cups and bake until set.

10. Smoked Salmon Breakfast Wrap:

Ingredients:

- Whole wheat wrap

- Smoked salmon

- Cream cheese

- Sliced cucumber

- Red onion

Instructions:

- Spread cream cheese on the wrap.

- Lay smoked salmon on top.

- Add sliced cucumber and red onion.

- Roll up and enjoy.

11. Peanut Butter Banana Toast:

Ingredients:

- Whole wheat bread

- Peanut butter

- Banana

- Honey

Instructions:

- Toast the bread.

- Spread peanut butter on the toast.

- Slice banana and arrange on top.

- Drizzle honey over the banana.

12. Veggie Omelette:

Ingredients:

- Eggs

- Chopped vegetables (bell peppers, onions, mushrooms, etc.)

- Cheese (optional)

- Salt and pepper

Instructions:

- Beat eggs and season with salt and pepper.

- Cook chopped vegetables in a pan.

- Pour eggs over the vegetables and cook until set.

- Add cheese before folding the omelette.

13. Banana Protein Pancakes:

Ingredients:

- Ripe bananas

- Eggs

- Protein powder

- Baking powder

- Vanilla extract

Instructions:

- Mash bananas in a bowl.

- Mix in eggs, protein powder, baking powder, and vanilla extract.

- Cook the batter on a heated non-stick pan to make pancakes.

14. Overnight Protein Oats:

Ingredients:

- Rolled oats

- Protein powder

- Chopped nuts

- Berries

- Milk or yogurt

Instructions:

- Mix oats, protein powder, and milk or yogurt in a jar.

- Refrigerate overnight.

- Top with chopped nuts and berries before eating.

15. Breakfast Quinoa Bowl:

Ingredients:

- Cooked quinoa

- Sliced almonds

- Fresh berries

- Honey

- Greek yogurt

Instructions:

- Mix cooked quinoa with sliced almonds.

- Top with fresh berries and a drizzle of honey.

- Serve with a dollop of Greek yogurt.

16. Tofu Scramble:

Ingredients:

- Tofu

- Chopped vegetables (bell peppers, onions, spinach, etc.)

- Turmeric

- Nutritional yeast (optional)

- Salt and pepper

Instructions:

• Crumble tofu with a fork.

• Sauté chopped vegetables in a pan.

• Add tofu, turmeric, nutritional yeast, salt, and pepper.

• Cook until heated through.

17. High-Protein Breakfast Bowl:

Ingredients:

• Cooked quinoa or brown rice

• Grilled chicken or turkey sausage

• Steamed broccoli

• Hummus

• Sunflower seeds

Instructions:

• Mix cooked quinoa or brown rice with grilled chicken or turkey sausage.

- Add steamed broccoli and a dollop of hummus.

- Sprinkle with sunflower seeds.

18. Chocolate Protein Overnight Oats:

Ingredients:

- Rolled oats

- Chocolate protein powder

- Chia seeds

- Almond milk

- Cocoa powder

- Banana slices

Instructions:

- Mix oats, chocolate protein powder, chia seeds, almond milk, and cocoa powder in a jar.

- Refrigerate overnight.

- Top with banana slices before eating.

19. Breakfast Quesadilla:

Ingredients:

• Whole wheat tortilla

• Scrambled eggs

• Shredded cheese

• Spinach

• Sliced tomatoes

Instructions:

• Place tortilla in a pan over medium heat.

• Layer scrambled eggs, shredded cheese, spinach, and sliced tomatoes on half of the tortilla.

• Fold the other half over to create a quesadilla.

• Cook until cheese melts and tortilla is crispy.

20. Pumpkin Protein Pancakes:

Ingredients:

- Canned pumpkin puree

- Eggs

- Oats

- Protein powder

- Pumpkin spice

- Maple syrup

Instructions:

- Blend pumpkin puree, eggs, oats, protein powder, and pumpkin spice in a blender.

- Cook the batter on a heated non-stick pan to make pancakes.

- Serve with a drizzle of maple syrup.

LUNCH

Grilled Chicken Salad:

Ingredients:

- Grilled chicken breast

- Mixed salad greens

- Cherry tomatoes

- Cucumber

- Red onion

- Balsamic vinaigrette

Instructions:

- Slice grilled chicken.

- Toss mixed salad greens, cherry tomatoes, cucumber, and red onion.

- Top with sliced chicken and drizzle with balsamic vinaigrette.

2. Lentil and Vegetable Soup:

Ingredients:

- Green or brown lentils

- Chopped vegetables (carrots, celery, onion, etc.)

- Vegetable broth

- Herbs (thyme, rosemary)

- Salt and pepper

Instructions:

- Cook lentils according to package instructions.

- Sauté chopped vegetables in a pot.

- Add cooked lentils, vegetable broth, herbs, salt, and pepper.

- Simmer until vegetables are tender.

3. Tuna Salad Wrap:

Ingredients:

- Canned tuna in water

- Greek yogurt

- Dijon mustard

- Chopped celery

- Red bell pepper

- Whole wheat wrap

Instructions:

- Mix canned tuna, Greek yogurt, Dijon mustard, chopped celery, and red bell pepper.

- Spread the mixture onto a whole wheat wrap.

- Roll up the wrap and enjoy.

4. Chickpea and Avocado Salad:

Ingredients:

- Cooked chickpeas

- Diced avocado

- Chopped cucumber

- Chopped red onion

- Fresh cilantro

- Lime juice

- Olive oil

- Salt and pepper

Instructions:

- Combine cooked chickpeas, diced avocado, chopped cucumber, red onion, and cilantro.

- Drizzle with lime juice and olive oil.

- Season with salt and pepper.

5. Quinoa Stuffed Bell Peppers:

Ingredients:

- Bell peppers

- Cooked quinoa

- Cooked ground turkey or black beans (for a vegetarian option)

- Chopped tomatoes

- Shredded cheese

- Spices (cumin, paprika, chili powder)

Instructions:

- Preheat the oven.

- Cut the tops off bell peppers and remove seeds.

- Mix cooked quinoa, ground turkey or black beans, chopped tomatoes, shredded cheese, and spices.

- Stuff the mixture into the bell peppers.

- Bake until peppers are tender and filling is heated through.

6. Turkey and Hummus Wrap:

Ingredients:

- Sliced turkey breast

- Hummus

- Baby spinach

- Sliced cucumber

- Whole wheat wrap

Instructions:

- Spread hummus onto a whole wheat wrap.

- Layer sliced turkey breast, baby spinach, and sliced cucumber.

- Roll up the wrap and enjoy.

7. Quinoa and Chicken Bowl:

Ingredients:

- Cooked quinoa

- Grilled chicken strips

- Steamed broccoli

- Sliced avocado

- Lemon tahini dressing

Instructions:

• Mix cooked quinoa, grilled chicken strips, steamed broccoli, and sliced avocado.

• Drizzle with lemon tahini dressing.

8. Greek Yogurt Chicken Salad:

Ingredients:

• Cooked shredded chicken

• Greek yogurt

• Diced celery

• Chopped red onion

• Dill

• Lemon juice

• Salt and pepper

Instructions:

• Mix cooked shredded chicken, Greek yogurt, diced celery, chopped red onion, dill, and lemon juice.

• Season with salt and pepper.

9. Spinach and Feta Stuffed Chicken Breast:

Ingredients:

• Chicken breast

• Spinach

• Crumbled feta cheese

• Garlic powder

• Paprika

• Salt and pepper

Instructions:

• Preheat the oven.

• Make a pocket in the chicken breast.

• Stuff with spinach and crumbled feta cheese.

• Sprinkle with garlic powder, paprika, salt, and pepper.

• Bake until chicken is cooked through.

10. Black Bean Quinoa Salad:

Ingredients:

• Cooked quinoa

• Black beans

• Corn kernels

• Diced red bell pepper

• Chopped cilantro

• Lime juice

• Olive oil

• Cumin

• Salt and pepper

Instructions:

- Mix cooked quinoa, black beans, corn kernels, diced red bell pepper, and chopped cilantro.

- Drizzle with lime juice and olive oil.

- Season with cumin, salt, and pepper.

11. Veggie and Egg Wrap:

Ingredients:

- Scrambled eggs

- Sautéed spinach

- Sliced tomatoes

- Sliced bell peppers

- Whole wheat wrap

Instructions:

- Fill a whole wheat wrap with scrambled eggs, sautéed spinach, sliced tomatoes, and sliced bell peppers.

- Roll up the wrap and enjoy.

12. Turkey and Quinoa Stuffed Peppers:

Ingredients:

- Bell peppers

- Cooked ground turkey

- Cooked quinoa

- Tomato sauce

- Shredded cheese

- Italian herbs (oregano, basil)

Instructions:

- Preheat the oven.

- Cut the tops off bell peppers and remove seeds.

- Mix cooked ground turkey, cooked quinoa, tomato sauce, shredded cheese, and Italian herbs.

- Stuff the mixture into the bell peppers.

• Bake until peppers are tender and filling is heated through.

13. Greek Chickpea Salad:

Ingredients:

• Cooked chickpeas

• Chopped cucumber

• Diced tomatoes

• Kalamata olives

• Crumbled feta cheese

• Red onion

• Greek dressing

Instructions:

• Mix cooked chickpeas, chopped cucumber, diced tomatoes, Kalamata olives, crumbled feta cheese, and red onion.

• Drizzle with Greek dressing.

14. Salmon and Quinoa Bowl:

Ingredients:

• Grilled salmon fillet

• Cooked quinoa

• Steamed asparagus

• Sliced avocado

• Lemon dill sauce

Instructions:

• Arrange grilled salmon fillet, cooked quinoa, steamed asparagus, and sliced avocado in a bowl.

• Drizzle with lemon dill sauce.

15. Tofu Stir-Fry:

Ingredients:

- Tofu, cubed

- Mixed stir-fry vegetables

- Soy sauce

- Ginger

- Garlic

- Sesame oil

Instructions:

- Sauté tofu cubes in a pan until golden brown.

- Add mixed stir-fry vegetables, soy sauce, ginger, and garlic.

- Drizzle with sesame oil and stir-fry until vegetables are tender.

16. Quinoa and Black Bean Bowl:

Ingredients:

- Cooked quinoa

- Black beans

- Sautéed onions and peppers

- Guacamole

- Salsa

- Lime wedges

Instructions:

- Mix cooked quinoa, black beans, sautéed onions and peppers.

- Top with guacamole and salsa.

- Serve with lime wedges.

17. Chicken and Vegetable Stir-Fry:

Ingredients:

- Sliced chicken breast

- Mixed stir-fry vegetables

- Stir-fry sauce

- Sesame seeds

- Green onions

Instructions:

- Sauté sliced chicken breast in a pan until cooked.

- Add mixed stir-fry vegetables and stir-fry sauce.

- Sprinkle with sesame seeds and chopped green onions.

18. Mediterranean Hummus Plate:

Ingredients:

- Hummus

- Grilled chicken strips

- Cherry tomatoes

- Cucumber slices

- Kalamata olives

- Feta cheese

- Pita bread or whole wheat crackers

Instructions:

- Arrange hummus, grilled chicken strips, cherry tomatoes, cucumber slices, Kalamata olives, and feta cheese on a plate.

- Serve with pita bread or whole wheat crackers.

19. Shrimp and Quinoa Salad:

Ingredients:

- Cooked shrimp

- Cooked quinoa

- Chopped bell peppers

- Chopped cucumber

- Chopped parsley

- Lemon vinaigrette

Instructions:

- Mix cooked shrimp, cooked quinoa, chopped bell peppers, chopped cucumber, and chopped parsley.

- Drizzle with lemon vinaigrette.

20. Vegetarian Bean Burrito:

Ingredients:

- Whole wheat tortilla

- Black beans or pinto beans

- Cooked brown rice

- Sautéed bell peppers and onions

- Salsa

- Shredded cheese

- Sour cream (optional)

Instructions:

- Warm the whole wheat tortilla.

- Fill with black beans or pinto beans, cooked brown rice, sautéed bell peppers and onions.

- Top with salsa, shredded cheese, and sour cream if desired.

- Roll up the tortilla and enjoy.

DINNER

Grilled Chicken Breast with Quinoa and Roasted Vegetables:

Ingredients:

- Chicken breast

- Quinoa

- Assorted vegetables (such as broccoli, carrots, bell peppers)

- Olive oil

- Herbs and spices (rosemary, thyme, garlic powder)

- Lemon juice

Instructions:

• Marinate chicken with herbs, spices, and lemon juice.

• Grill the chicken until cooked through.

• Prepare quinoa according to package instructions.

• Toss vegetables with olive oil and roast in the oven.

• Serve grilled chicken with quinoa and roasted vegetables.

2. Baked Salmon with Brown Rice and Steamed Asparagus:

Ingredients:

• Salmon fillet

• Brown rice

• Asparagus

• Olive oil

- Lemon

- Garlic

- Herbs (dill, parsley)

- Salt and pepper

Instructions:

- Preheat oven and line a baking sheet.

- Place salmon fillet on the baking sheet, drizzle with lemon juice, olive oil, and herbs.

- Bake salmon until cooked.

- Cook brown rice according to package instructions.

- Steam asparagus until tender.

- Serve baked salmon with brown rice and steamed asparagus.

3. Turkey and Quinoa Stuffed Bell Peppers:

Ingredients:

- Bell peppers

- Ground turkey

- Cooked quinoa

- Tomato sauce

- Onion

- Garlic

- Herbs (oregano, basil)

- Shredded cheese

Instructions:

- Preheat oven.

- Sauté onion and garlic, add ground turkey and cook until browned.

- Mix cooked quinoa, tomato sauce, herbs, and half of the shredded cheese with the turkey mixture.

- Cut the tops off bell peppers, remove seeds, and stuff with the mixture.

- Top with the remaining shredded cheese.

- Bake until peppers are tender and filling is heated through.

4. Beef Stir-Fry with Broccoli and Brown Rice:

Ingredients:

- Beef strips

- Broccoli florets

- Brown rice

- Soy sauce

- Ginger

- Garlic

- Sesame oil

- Red pepper flakes (optional)

Instructions:

• Marinate beef strips with soy sauce, ginger, and garlic.

• Heat a pan and stir-fry beef until browned.

• Add broccoli and cook until tender-crisp.

• Season with sesame oil and red pepper flakes.

• Serve beef stir-fry over cooked brown rice.

5. Lentil and Chickpea Curry:

Ingredients:

• Cooked lentils

• Cooked chickpeas

• Onion

• Garlic

• Tomatoes

• Curry spices (turmeric, cumin, coriander)

- Coconut milk

- Fresh cilantro

Instructions:

- Sauté onion and garlic in a pot.

- Add tomatoes and curry spices, cook until tomatoes are soft.

- Stir in cooked lentils, chickpeas, and coconut milk.

- Simmer until flavors meld.

- Serve over rice and garnish with fresh cilantro.

6. Grilled Tofu and Vegetable Skewers:

Ingredients:

- Tofu, cubed

- Assorted vegetables (bell peppers, zucchini, mushrooms)

- Olive oil

- Lemon juice

- Herbs (oregano, thyme)

- Salt and pepper

Instructions:

- Thread tofu and vegetables onto skewers.

- Whisk together olive oil, lemon juice, herbs, salt, and pepper.

- Brush skewers with the mixture.

- Grill skewers until tofu is lightly browned and vegetables are tender.

7. Shrimp and Avocado Salad:

Ingredients:

- Cooked shrimp

- Mixed salad greens

- Avocado

- Cherry tomatoes

- Red onion

- Cilantro

- Lime vinaigrette

Instructions:

- Toss mixed salad greens, cooked shrimp, diced avocado, cherry tomatoes, chopped red onion, and cilantro.

- Drizzle with lime vinaigrette.

8. Chicken and Broccoli Alfredo:

Ingredients:

- Grilled chicken strips

- Cooked whole wheat fettuccine

- Broccoli florets

- Alfredo sauce (lightened with Greek yogurt)

• Parmesan cheese

• Black pepper

Instructions:

• Cook whole wheat fettuccine according to package instructions.

• Steam broccoli until tender.

• Heat grilled chicken strips.

• Mix cooked fettuccine, broccoli, chicken, and Alfredo sauce.

• Serve with a sprinkle of Parmesan cheese and black pepper.

9. Quinoa and Black Bean Bowl with Guacamole:

Ingredients:

• Cooked quinoa

• Black beans

- Sautéed bell peppers and onions

- Guacamole

- Salsa

- Lime wedges

Instructions:

- Mix cooked quinoa, black beans, sautéed bell peppers and onions.

- Top with guacamole and salsa.

- Serve with lime wedges.

10. Baked Chicken Thighs with Sweet Potato and Brussels Sprouts:

Ingredients:

- Chicken thighs

- Sweet potatoes, cubed

- Brussels sprouts, halved

- Olive oil

- Garlic powder

- Paprika

- Rosemary

- Salt and pepper

Instructions:

- Preheat oven.

- Toss sweet potatoes and Brussels sprouts with olive oil, garlic powder, paprika, rosemary, salt, and pepper.

- Arrange chicken thighs on the same baking sheet.

- Bake until chicken is cooked through and vegetables are tender.

11. Seared Tuna Steak with Quinoa and Asparagus:

Ingredients:

- Tuna steak

- Cooked quinoa

- Asparagus

- Lemon

- Olive oil

- Soy sauce

- Sesame seeds

Instructions:

- Heat a pan and sear tuna steak on both sides.

- Cook asparagus in the same pan.

- Mix cooked quinoa with lemon juice, olive oil, and soy sauce.

- Serve seared tuna steak with quinoa and asparagus.

- Sprinkle with sesame seeds.

12. Veggie-Packed Egg Frittata:

Ingredients:

• Eggs

• Chopped vegetables (bell peppers, spinach, onions, etc.)

• Cheese (optional)

• Herbs (thyme, oregano)

• Salt and pepper

Instructions:

• Preheat oven.

• Whisk eggs, add chopped vegetables, cheese, herbs, salt, and pepper.

• Pour mixture into a greased baking dish.

• Bake until the frittata is set and golden brown.

13. Blackened Salmon with Quinoa and Steamed Green Beans:

Ingredients:

• Salmon fillet

• Cooked quinoa

• Green beans

• Cajun seasoning

• Olive oil

• Lemon

Instructions:

• Rub Cajun seasoning on both sides of the salmon fillet.

• Heat a pan with olive oil and cook the salmon.

• Steam green beans until tender.

• Serve blackened salmon with quinoa and steamed green beans.

• Squeeze lemon juice over the salmon.

14. Stuffed Portobello Mushrooms with Spinach and Goat Cheese:

Ingredients:

• Portobello mushrooms

• Sautéed spinach

• Goat cheese

• Garlic

• Olive oil

• Balsamic vinegar

• Herbs (thyme, rosemary)

Instructions:

• Preheat oven.

• Remove the stems from Portobello mushrooms.

- Brush mushrooms with olive oil and balsamic vinegar.

- Fill with sautéed spinach, goat cheese, garlic, and herbs.

- Bake until mushrooms are tender and cheese is melted.

15. Teriyaki Tofu Stir-Fry:

Ingredients:

- Tofu, cubed

- Mixed stir-fry vegetables

- Teriyaki sauce

- Ginger

- Garlic

- Sesame oil

Instructions:

- Sauté tofu cubes in a pan until golden brown.

- Add mixed stir-fry vegetables, teriyaki sauce, ginger, and garlic.

- Drizzle with sesame oil and stir-fry until vegetables are tender.

16. BBQ Chicken Quinoa Bowl:

Ingredients:

- Grilled chicken breast, sliced

- Cooked quinoa

- Black beans

- Corn kernels

- BBQ sauce

- Avocado

- Fresh cilantro

Instructions:

• Mix cooked quinoa, black beans, and corn kernels.

• Toss sliced grilled chicken with BBQ sauce.

• Serve chicken over quinoa mixture and top with sliced avocado and fresh cilantro.

17. Veggie and Lentil Stir-Fry:

Ingredients:

• Cooked green or brown lentils

• Mixed stir-fry vegetables

• Soy sauce

• Garlic

• Ginger

• Sesame oil

Instructions:

• Sauté mixed stir-fry vegetables with garlic and ginger.

• Add cooked lentils and soy sauce.

• Drizzle with sesame oil and stir-fry until everything is well combined.

18. Lemon Herb Grilled Shrimp with Couscous and Roasted Vegetables:

Ingredients:

• Grilled shrimp

• Cooked couscous

• Roasted vegetables (zucchini, bell peppers, onions)

• Lemon juice

• Olive oil

• Fresh herbs (parsley, basil)

Instructions:

• Toss grilled shrimp with lemon juice and fresh herbs.

• Mix cooked couscous with roasted vegetables.

• Serve shrimp over couscous and vegetables.

19. Veggie-Packed Chicken Quesadillas:

Ingredients:

• Grilled chicken strips

• Whole wheat tortillas

• Sautéed vegetables (bell peppers, onions, mushrooms)

• Shredded cheese

• Guacamole

• Greek yogurt (as a sour cream alternative)

Instructions:

• Lay a tortilla on a pan over medium heat.

• Layer grilled chicken strips, sautéed vegetables, and shredded cheese.

- Top with another tortilla and cook until cheese melts.

- Serve with guacamole and a dollop of Greek yogurt.

20. Baked Cod with Quinoa and Sautéed Spinach:

Ingredients:

- Cod fillet

- Cooked quinoa

- Sautéed spinach

- Lemon

- Olive oil

- Garlic

- Herbs (thyme, rosemary)

- Salt and pepper

Instructions:

- Preheat oven.

- Place cod fillet on a baking sheet, drizzle with lemon juice, olive oil, garlic, herbs, salt, and pepper.

- Bake until cod is flaky and cooked through.

- Serve cod with cooked quinoa and sautéed spinach.

SNACKS

Greek Yogurt Parfait:

Ingredients:

- Greek yogurt

- Mixed berries (blueberries, strawberries, raspberries)

- Honey

- Granola (optional)

Instructions:

- In a glass or bowl, layer Greek yogurt.

- Add a layer of mixed berries.

- Drizzle with honey.

- Repeat the layers if desired.

- Top with granola for added crunch.

2. Cottage Cheese and Fruit Bowl:

Ingredients:

- Cottage cheese

- Sliced peaches, pineapple, or other fruits

- Nuts or seeds (walnuts, almonds, chia seeds)

- Honey (optional)

Instructions:

- Spoon cottage cheese into a bowl.

- Add sliced fruits and nuts or seeds.

- Drizzle with honey if desired.

3. Hard-Boiled Eggs with Hummus:

Ingredients:

• Hard-boiled eggs

• Hummus

• Paprika or chili powder (for sprinkling)

Instructions:

• Peel the hard-boiled eggs.

• Serve with a side of hummus for dipping.

• Sprinkle with paprika or chili powder for added flavor.

4. Peanut Butter Banana Toast:

Ingredients:

• Whole wheat toast

• Peanut butter

• Banana slices

• Chia seeds (optional)

Instructions:

• Toast the whole wheat bread.

• Spread peanut butter on the toast.

• Top with banana slices.

• Sprinkle with chia seeds for extra texture and nutrients.

5. Roasted Chickpeas:

Ingredients:

• Canned chickpeas (garbanzo beans)

• Olive oil

• Seasonings (paprika, cumin, garlic powder, salt)

Instructions:

• Preheat oven.

• Drain and rinse chickpeas, then pat dry.

- Toss chickpeas with olive oil and seasonings.

- Roast in the oven until crispy.

6. Almond Butter Rice Cakes:

Ingredients:

- Rice cakes

- Almond butter

- Sliced banana or apple

- Cinnamon

Instructions:

- Spread almond butter on rice cakes.

- Top with sliced banana or apple.

- Sprinkle with cinnamon for extra flavor.

7. Greek Yogurt and Fruit Smoothie:

Ingredients:

- Greek yogurt

- Mixed berries (blueberries, strawberries, raspberries)

- Banana

- Spinach (optional)

- Milk or water

Instructions:

- Blend Greek yogurt, mixed berries, banana, and spinach (if using).

- Add milk or water to reach desired consistency.

8. Trail Mix:

Ingredients:

- Mixed nuts (almonds, cashews, walnuts)

- Dried fruits (raisins, cranberries, apricots)

- Dark chocolate chips (optional)

Instructions:

• Mix nuts, dried fruits, and dark chocolate chips (if using).

• Portion into snack-sized bags for easy grabbing.

9. Veggie Sticks with Hummus:

Ingredients:

• Carrot sticks

• Celery sticks

• Bell pepper strips

• Hummus

Instructions:

• Wash and cut veggies into sticks.

• Serve with hummus for dipping.

10. Chocolate Protein Balls:

Ingredients:

- Protein powder (whey or plant-based)

- Nut butter (peanut butter, almond butter)

- Rolled oats

- Honey or maple syrup

- Dark chocolate chips

Instructions:

- Mix protein powder, nut butter, rolled oats, and sweetener.

- Roll into bite-sized balls.

- Melt dark chocolate chips and drizzle over the balls.

11. Turkey and Cheese Roll-Ups:

Ingredients:

- Deli turkey slices

- Cheese slices

- Mustard or mayonnaise (optional)

Instructions:

- Lay turkey slices flat.

- Place a cheese slice on each turkey slice.

- Add a thin layer of mustard or mayonnaise if desired.

- Roll up and enjoy.

12. Edamame Snack:

Ingredients:

- Edamame (soybeans), steamed and salted

Instructions:

- Steam edamame according to package instructions.

• Sprinkle with salt and enjoy the beans by popping them out of the pods.

13. Greek Yogurt Dip with Veggies:

Ingredients:

• Greek yogurt

• Dill or other herbs

• Mixed vegetables (carrot sticks, cucumber slices, cherry tomatoes)

Instructions:

• Mix Greek yogurt with dill or your preferred herbs.

• Use as a dip for the mixed vegetables.

14. Chia Seed Pudding:

Ingredients:

• Chia seeds

- Milk (dairy or plant-based)

- Vanilla extract

- Honey or maple syrup

- Fresh fruits

Instructions:

- Mix chia seeds, milk, vanilla extract, and sweetener.

- Refrigerate overnight until thickened.

- Top with fresh fruits before eating.

15. Apple Slices with Nut Butter:

Ingredients:

- Apple slices

- Nut butter (peanut butter, almond butter)

Instructions:

- Slice an apple.

- Spread nut butter on apple slices.

- Enjoy the apple slices with nut butter.

SMOOTHIES

Berry Protein Blast:

Ingredients:

- Frozen mixed berries

- Greek yogurt

- Protein powder (whey or plant-based)

- Spinach (optional)

- Water or milk (dairy or plant-based)

Instructions:

- Blend frozen mixed berries, Greek yogurt, protein powder, spinach (if using), and water or milk until smooth.

2. Peanut Butter Banana Protein Smoothie:

Ingredients:

• Banana

• Peanut butter

• Protein powder

• Oats

• Milk (dairy or plant-based)

Instructions:

• Blend banana, peanut butter, protein powder, oats, and milk until creamy.

3. Chocolate Almond Protein Shake:

Ingredients:

• Almond milk

• Chocolate protein powder

• Almond butter

- Banana

- Ice cubes

Instructions:

- Blend almond milk, chocolate protein powder, almond butter, banana, and ice cubes until well combined.

4. Green Protein Power Smoothie:

Ingredients:

- Spinach

- Banana

- Greek yogurt

- Protein powder

- Chia seeds

- Water or coconut water

Instructions:

• Blend spinach, banana, Greek yogurt, protein powder, chia seeds, and water or coconut water until smooth.

5. Tropical Mango Protein Smoothie:

Ingredients:

• Frozen mango chunks

• Pineapple chunks

• Greek yogurt

• Protein powder

• Coconut water

Instructions:

• Blend frozen mango chunks, pineapple chunks, Greek yogurt, protein powder, and coconut water until creamy.

6. Vanilla Berry Protein Smoothie:

Ingredients:

• Mixed berries (blueberries, strawberries, raspberries)

• Vanilla protein powder

• Almond milk

• Chia seeds

Instructions:

• Blend mixed berries, vanilla protein powder, almond milk, and chia seeds until well blended.

7. Mocha Protein Shake:

Ingredients:

• Coffee (cooled)

• Chocolate protein powder

• Almond milk

• Banana

- Ice cubes

Instructions:

- Blend coffee, chocolate protein powder, almond milk, banana, and ice cubes until smooth.

8. Spinach and Avocado Protein Smoothie:

Ingredients:

- Spinach

- Avocado

- Banana

- Protein powder

- Almond milk

- Water

Instructions:

- Blend spinach, avocado, banana, protein powder, almond milk, and water until creamy.

9. Blueberry Oatmeal Protein Smoothie:

Ingredients:

• Frozen blueberries

• Rolled oats

• Greek yogurt

• Protein powder

• Almond milk

Instructions:

• Blend frozen blueberries, rolled oats, Greek yogurt, protein powder, and almond milk until smooth.

10. Pumpkin Spice Protein Smoothie:

Ingredients:

• Canned pumpkin puree

- Protein powder

- Almond milk

- Banana

- Pumpkin spice

Instructions:

- Blend canned pumpkin puree, protein powder, almond milk, banana, and pumpkin spice until well combined.

11. Strawberry Banana Protein Shake:

Ingredients:

- Strawberries

- Banana

- Protein powder

- Greek yogurt

- Water or milk

Instructions:

• Blend strawberries, banana, protein powder, Greek yogurt, and water or milk until creamy.

12. Chocolate Peanut Butter Protein Smoothie:

Ingredients:

• Chocolate protein powder

• Peanut butter

• Banana

• Almond milk

• Ice cubes

Instructions:

• Blend chocolate protein powder, peanut butter, banana, almond milk, and ice cubes until smooth.

13. Coconut Mango Protein Smoothie:

Ingredients:

- Frozen mango chunks

- Coconut milk

- Vanilla protein powder

- Coconut flakes

Instructions:

- Blend frozen mango chunks, coconut milk, vanilla protein powder, and coconut flakes until creamy.

14. Almond Joy Protein Shake:

Ingredients:

- Almond milk

- Chocolate protein powder

- Almond butter

- Coconut flakes

• Almonds

Instructions:

• Blend almond milk, chocolate protein powder, almond butter, coconut flakes, and almonds until well blended.

15. Peachy Green Protein Smoothie:

Ingredients:

• Peach slices (fresh or frozen)

• Spinach

• Greek yogurt

• Protein powder

• Water or coconut water

Instructions:

• Blend peach slices, spinach, Greek yogurt, protein powder, and water or coconut water until smooth.

DESSERTS

Chocolate Protein Mug Cake:

Ingredients:

- Chocolate protein powder

- Almond flour

- Cocoa powder

- Baking powder

- Egg

- Almond milk

- Dark chocolate chips (optional)

Instructions:

- In a mug, mix chocolate protein powder, almond flour, cocoa powder, and baking powder.

- Add egg and almond milk, and mix until smooth.

- Fold in dark chocolate chips.

• Microwave for 1-2 minutes until the cake is cooked through.

2. Peanut Butter Protein Bars:

Ingredients:

• Peanut butter

• Protein powder (vanilla or chocolate)

• Rolled oats

• Honey

• Dark chocolate chips (for drizzling)

Instructions:

• Mix peanut butter, protein powder, rolled oats, and honey.

• Press the mixture into a baking pan and refrigerate until firm.

• Melt dark chocolate chips and drizzle over the bars.

3. Greek Yogurt Parfait with Nuts and Berries:

Ingredients:

• Greek yogurt

• Mixed nuts (almonds, walnuts)

• Mixed berries (blueberries, raspberries, strawberries)

• Honey (optional)

Instructions:

• In a glass, layer Greek yogurt, mixed nuts, mixed berries, and repeat.

• Drizzle with honey for added sweetness.

4. Protein-Packed Chocolate Pudding:

Ingredients:

• Silken tofu

- Chocolate protein powder

- Cocoa powder

- Vanilla extract

- Maple syrup or honey

Instructions:

- Blend silken tofu, chocolate protein powder, cocoa powder, vanilla extract, and sweetener until smooth.

- Chill in the refrigerator before serving.

5. Cottage Cheese Berry Bowl:

Ingredients:

- Cottage cheese

- Mixed berries (blueberries, strawberries, raspberries)

- Nuts or seeds (walnuts, chia seeds)

- Honey

Instructions:

- In a bowl, layer cottage cheese, mixed berries, nuts or seeds, and honey.

6. Chocolate Peanut Butter Protein Balls:

Ingredients:

- Chocolate protein powder

- Peanut butter

- Rolled oats

- Honey

- Dark chocolate chips (for coating)

Instructions:

- Mix chocolate protein powder, peanut butter, rolled oats, and honey.

- Roll into bite-sized balls.

• Melt dark chocolate chips and dip the balls for a coating.

7. Vanilla Protein Pancakes:

Ingredients:

• Vanilla protein powder

• Oats

• Greek yogurt

• Egg

• Baking powder

• Vanilla extract

• Maple syrup (for topping)

Instructions:

• Blend vanilla protein powder, oats, Greek yogurt, egg, baking powder, and vanilla extract.

- Cook the batter on a non-stick pan to make pancakes.

- Top with a drizzle of maple syrup.

8. Chocolate Protein Ice Cream:

Ingredients:

- Frozen bananas

- Chocolate protein powder

- Almond milk

- Cocoa powder

- Dark chocolate chips (optional)

Instructions:

- Blend frozen bananas, chocolate protein powder, almond milk, and cocoa powder until creamy.

- Fold in dark chocolate chips if desired.

- Freeze for a firmer texture.

9. Chia Seed Protein Pudding:

Ingredients:

• Chia seeds

• Almond milk

• Protein powder (vanilla or chocolate)

• Vanilla extract

• Berries (for topping)

Instructions:

• Mix chia seeds, almond milk, protein powder, and vanilla extract.

• Refrigerate overnight until thickened.

• Top with berries before serving.

10. Protein-Packed Chocolate Mousse:

Ingredients:

- Avocado

- Chocolate protein powder

- Cocoa powder

- Maple syrup or honey

- Vanilla extract

Instructions:

- Blend avocado, chocolate protein powder, cocoa powder, sweetener, and vanilla extract until smooth.

- Chill in the refrigerator before serving.

11. Almond Butter Protein Cookies:

Ingredients:

- Almond butter

- Protein powder (vanilla or chocolate)

- Rolled oats

- Egg

- Honey or maple syrup

- Dark chocolate chips (optional)

Instructions:

- Mix almond butter, protein powder, rolled oats, egg, and sweetener.

- Fold in dark chocolate chips.

- Shape into cookies and bake until golden.

CONCLUSION

A protein-rich diet cookbook is a valuable resource for individuals seeking to enhance their overall health, support muscle growth, manage weight, and maintain satiety. This type of cookbook offers a diverse range of recipes that are not only delicious but also packed with protein-rich ingredients. By incorporating these recipes into your daily meals, you can ensure that you're meeting your protein needs while enjoying a variety of flavors and dishes.

A well-structured protein-rich diet can provide numerous benefits, including improved muscle recovery, increased metabolism, and better control over hunger and cravings. It can also be beneficial for athletes, individuals engaged in strength training, and those looking to manage or prevent certain health conditions.

When creating or following a protein-rich diet cookbook, it's important to consider a balanced approach that includes a variety of protein sources, such as lean meats, poultry, fish, eggs, dairy products, legumes, nuts, and seeds. Additionally, pairing protein with other nutrient-rich foods like vegetables, whole grains, and healthy fats can contribute to a well-rounded and nutritious eating plan.

Remember to personalize your protein-rich diet based on your individual dietary preferences, fitness goals, and any specific nutritional requirements you may have. Consulting a healthcare professional or registered dietitian can provide tailored guidance to ensure that your protein-rich diet is both effective and safe for your unique needs.

Incorporating a protein-rich diet cookbook into your culinary repertoire can make achieving your health and fitness goals an enjoyable and flavorful journey. Whether you're aiming to build muscle, support your active lifestyle, or simply make more mindful dietary choices, a protein-rich diet cookbook can be a valuable tool to help you along the way.

Printed in Great Britain
by Amazon

42522399R00056